W. G. B. 09-0

21 - 10 - 1962.

£4-00

# The Students Gallery

## DUTCH PAINTING

# DUTCH PAINTING

## BY PIERRE DESCARGUES

*with 46 colour plates*

THAMES AND HUDSON

LONDON

TRANSLATED FROM THE FRENCH
BY STUART HOOD

© THAMES AND HUDSON LONDON 1959
SECOND IMPRESSION 1961
PRINTED IN GERMANY BY CARL SCHÜNEMANN BREMEN
THIS BOOK IS PUBLISHED IN FRANCE BY
EDITIONS AIMERY SOMOGY PARIS

# LIST OF COLOUR PLATES

HOW much interest is there today in those small dark paintings of grotesque, reeling drunkards? – or in those others which show a military gallant, an old doctor, a young patient or a handsome flirtatious young man conversing like actors in a play? In fact the artist of today is more interested in the decorative work of the Italians than in the anecdotal paintings of the Dutch. He regards with distrust canvasses with such titles as 'When the cat's away, the mice will play' or 'After drinking' or 'A Mother's Task,' for the reason that, in the 19th century, so much bad painting was motivated by good and praiseworthy sentiments of this very kind. Art has with such difficulty shed the role of amiable satirist and discreet universal entertainer, that, looking down from their exalted position of unyielding independence, modern artists reject any element in a picture which might be considered 'literary' – that is to say, any attempt to tell a story.

Of Dutch 17th-century painting, they wish to retain only Rembrandt and Vermeer – the former for his mysterious quality, the latter for his composition and colour. And if Frans Hals is the only portrait painter of the age who finds favour in their eyes, perhaps it is because of the cruelty with which he mocked the City Councillors of Haarlem. Of the landscapists, Ruisdael and Hobbema are no longer as highly praised as they used to be. Savery and Hercules Seghers are being rediscovered, but this is merely a just re-evaluation of talents hitherto hidden among the ranks of second-rate artists. And as for the animal painters, is anyone proud of having on his walls a cow by Paulus Potter or a horse by Wouwerman?

Today, with the exception of men of incomparable genius, such as Rembrandt or Vermeer, Dutch painting is neglected. Present-day art does not touch the same chords. Perhaps in a few years' time, however, a sky by Ruisdael will cause the same excitement as a Cézanne apple for which vast sums are bid and counterbid. Thanks to the Impressionists, who reminded us of the existence of Boudin and Jongkind, we shall perhaps rediscover the Barbizon school, and from there the Dutch landscapists. Perhaps Jongkind will lead us to rediscover Averkamp. And Pieter de Hooch, whom we tolerate only because of Vermeer, may even introduce us to Ostade. Be that as it may, we still regard Dutch painting of the Golden Age as a curiosity which is completely irrelevant to the art of our times.

However, this detachment, this distance, undoubtedly provides a good vantage point for discovering the exceptional, the revolutionary qualities which Dutch Art represented in its day.

In its early stages Dutch art has all the characteristics of a new, revolutionary art – crudity for instance, and lack of refinement, not to mention lack of freedom and intelligence. We can imagine what the Italians, familiar with their gods and goddesses, the French, who so liked the sumptuous portraits of their Princes and the Flemings with their craze for tables piled high with food – veritable orgies of painting – must have thought of these mass-produced, stereotyped portraits of grave burghers clad in austere black, or of those scenes which show a draper, a fishmonger or an apothecary dressed up as soldiers and parading their potbellies through the streets of their towns. We can safely assume that they laughed; just as today, we are surprised to find that the citizens of Amsterdam preferred the pallid pupil to his great independent master, that they fêted Gerard Dou and abandoned Rembrandt as soon as he began to paint subjects other than his fashionable portraits. But Dutch painting is not limited to the two or three men of genius thrown up by the Golden Age. It also includes that long line of portraits and genre pictures through which a whole nation became aware of its unity. Dutch art represents an exceptional period in the history of Art.

At the beginning of the century, in 1609, Philip II of Spain, worn out by an exhausting war and by the guerrilla compaign against him, was compelled to grant his Low Country provinces a twelve-year truce. Thirty years later, in 1648 at Münster, Philip IV was forced to recognise the final independence of his former subjects. This was the ultimate victory, the complete triumph of a small nation which had been in a state of revolution and war since 1566. The herring-fishers of Holland and the Princes of the

House of Orange had fought without respite first against Charles V and Austria, and subsequently against the Spaniards. In fact, these provinces had never been completely conquered. Spanish soldiers and Dutch serving-girls had perhaps cooperated to produce an astonishing mixture of races, but the old dream of independence had never left the towns which had grown used to their privileges as free cities. It was the ideas of the Reformation which touched off the explosion.

'Thou shalt not turn towards graven images.' That short sentence from Leviticus fired the iconoclasts of 1566 in their assault on the Catholic churches. They sacked sculptures, altar paintings and stained-glass windows. It was then that Philip II ordered the terrible Duke of Alba to bring the heretics back to reason. But their ranks were soon swelled by revolutionaries; for Protestants and Catholics came to terms in certain districts of the territory in order to proclaim the Republic in 1581. This Republic was to lead to the federation of seven provinces, for the Dutch were intent on the medieval ideal of the free merchant city, which links itself with other equally free cities to increase its own strength and to safeguard its trade. The Duke of Alba's repressive measures were pitiless: it was war, a war without mercy, at once religious and national. The fight was waged against both the occupying forces and their religion. To kill a Spaniard was to kill a Papist.

Thus Dutch painting begins with a great bonfire of works of art. It may be said to have been born out of this destruction. Amsterdam, Utrecht, Delft, the Hague, Leyden burned and destroyed the treasures of their churches. But were these Dutch works of art? The idea of Dutch art was not yet born, and the real artistic centres had not yet left Bruges and Antwerp and moved beyond the frontiers of Flanders. Bruges and Antwerp remained in the hands of the Catholics, and Dutch artists were to find themselves completely isolated. The boat which carried the French or German traveller to Dordrecht and Nijmegen, the gates to the United Provinces, did not merely prove to him that he was entering another country, that he was passing into a new land between sea and sky; it was the link between two completely different worlds.

11

The traveller might have expected a country that was weakened – ruined for a whole century like Germany at the end of the Thirty Years War. On the contrary, Holland was living through its most prosperous and glorious years. The *gueux* who had brought the uprising of 1566 to a successful conclusion were more fortunate than the German knights and peasants who had been massacred in a similar battle forty years earlier. *Their* sons were the richest men in the world. According to Wicquefort: 'Norway was their forest; the banks of the Rhine, the Garonne, and the Dordogne, their vineyards; Prussia and Poland, their granaries; India and Arabia, their gardens.' The good burghers ruled in the islands of the Straits, in Curaçao and Guiana thanks to their fleet of twenty thousand ships. They owned concessions in China and Japan, occupied Ceylon and the Cape, and founded New Amsterdam, which was to become New York. Their bank in Amsterdam acted as money-lender to the whole world. They expanded their cities, built towers and houses, and opened new factories to provide employment for the Protestant workers from the southern provinces who had come to seek refuge and work. Everything in the country was new. The merchants had installed themselves in the hastily whitewashed churches and the students in the convents; one even saw riding schools exercising in the cloisters. We can easily imagine the ardour of a whole nation thirsting to participate in this transformation of its life and build the society born of the Revolution. Nationalism, at its inception, is always uncompromising; very quickly it leads a country to desire a completely self-sufficient life.

The Dutch quickly developed an architecture of their own, which was very different from that of the Flemings. Enamoured of freedom, they welcomed intellectuals of other countries, publishing their subversive writing; in a century when the press was very closely supervised, they were the owners of the largest newspapers. It was after all Spinoza who said: 'The purpose and final aim of the State is liberty.'

As for their painting, of which there many more examples than of sculpture – for against that every Protestant still felt in the depths of his heart a stirring of iconoclastic rage – it was to be entirely original in form.

That is to say that this Golden Age was to be a century of enrichment and renewal for the Low Countries.

The painter could therefore no longer paint God; Rembrandt was the exception to the rule. They painted Man. Carel van Mander, the Vasari of the North, notes this transformation of the arts – not without a touch of melancholy: 'The painters dreamed of ambitious fictions; instead, they were forced to paint portraits.' The period of mysticism which compelled the Spanish kings to build Escorials in the desert, the better to prepare themselves for their dialogue with Christ, was over and done with. Religion was almost becoming a code of morals.

The Prince or Burgomaster, who could no longer have himself depicted by some salaried painter at the side of the Saint of his choice, had himself painted in company, carrying out a good work, or in the pursuit of his profession. To rediscover today something of that social life which the Dutch considered one of man's accomplishments we must go to Switzerland, that country of dining clubs, of innumerable Societies, where each citizen is armed and takes part in military exercises as did, in Holland, the archers, halbardiers and musketeers of the Civil Guard whose duty it was to go the rounds of their cities.

In France and Spain, the Catholics Georges de La Tour and Valdès Léal painted works of meditation on death and on God. In Holland, Frans Hals depicted banqueting archers.

The painters, then, were the most valuable of allies in the national enterprise of glorifying the good citizen. They painted portraits of cloth merchants, butchers, doctors and newly-rich farmers; they painted whatever their clients wanted – their favourite landscape, their tables groaning with food and their animals. They depicted the people of the towns and their austere churches, denuded of any ornament except flags taken from the Spaniards. And in their scenes from peasant life, in their inn scenes and their fairground frolics, perhaps they were rendering homage to the memory of those bumpkins, the *gueux*, who had made the Revolution. Society could not be better served.

The trade in painting flourished. Each town had its merchants who displayed pictures in their houses; but paintings could also be bought in a shop or even in the markets or from hawkers. As today, painters were under contract. As today, numerous collectors spent their time buying and selling pictures. As today, canvasses were offered for sale at public auctions and every middle-class or peasant house was decorated with numerous paintings. It was quite different in Italy, where the artists were working on large mural decorations or were dependent on patrons. The walls of the Protestant churches remained bare. Dutch painters could count only on orders for portraits or group paintings.

This extolling of the 'bourgeois,' this glorification of humdrum daily life, led to a realism which was certainly new and revolutionary; naturally it had not sprung to life, fully developed, with the new century. Its sources, both natural and foreign, are obvious.

After the iconoclasts had passed there naturally remained very little which could provide a basis for the experiments of the new painters. We know that, far from rejecting their predecessors, they professed a deep admiration for the fragments of works of art which had been carefully reassembled after the cataclysm. Theirs was a sincere admiration. The historian Orlers reports that a large majority of the simple burghers who sat in council in the Town Hall of Leyden refused to sell a 'Last Judgment' by Lucas van Leyden to the Emperor Rudolph II. And this in spite of the fact that the Sovereign offered to pay 'as many gold ducats as are needed to cover the painting.' Carel van Mander, for his part, is deeply moved by the wholesale destruction of the great paintings of Pieter Aertszen in 1566. He says the painter died of heartbreak. But the originality of such masters as Lucas van Leyden, who was mid-way between Dürer and the Italian painters, and Aertszen, a forerunner of Jordaens, must not be allowed to obscure the persistent influence on their works of medieval culture – a culture which today would be described as 'popular', – which expressed itself in symbols and parables. It was a world of secondary meanings in which Christ is the good shepherd, in which the virtues take on a human face, in which a hunter may become a purifying angel and a fisherman the instrument of a miracle – a world, reduced to simple actions

14

and simple people, suddenly illuminated by the Revelation. The peoples of the North were more eager than the Italians for stories such as these, at once crystal-clear and mysterious. The men who painted them, like Bosch and Breugel, arrived at a complicated symbolism whose meaning often escapes us and which poses embarrassing questions about beggars and cripples.

The ideas of the Renaissance dealt a fatal blow to this symbolism, but the taste for the subjects through which it expressed itself remained very much alive both in the painters and with the public. Hence, a kind of habit of painting scenes of popular life, a habit which was reinforced by a very common theme dear to militant Christianity, namely that of 'The Seven Good Works'. In it we are shown the men of good works ministering to the sick or dispensing charity. Thus the transition from the beggars of Hieronymus Bosch to the peasants of Averkamp becomes clear and the inn scenes of van Ostade are already there in Bosch's 'Prodigal Son' if only in the background of the paintings, and the theme of the gipsy story of the 'Good Adventure' which Honthorst of Utrecht found in Caravaggio's Roman studio was already to be found in Breugel's drawing. The evidence that portraits of humanists and studies of proportions in the Italian manner did not take up all the time of the 16th-century painters, and that they were capable of observing how people lived around them, is equally abundant.

Together with genre scenes and portraits, the still-life, the landscape and the animal scene are characteristic of Dutch 17th-century art. In these spheres, too, there existed some sort of Nordic tradition. Patenier was undoubtedly the first landscape painter in the modern sense of the word. Dürer, who was much appreciated in Flanders, etched a number of 'portraits' of horses and, like a modern scientist drawn to the spot by a coelacanth, rushed in vain to Zeeland in the hope of sketching a whale, which had just been discovered stranded on a beach. Finally it is thought that Antonello da Messina, a passionate admirer of Flemish art, first contracted in the North, before introducing it in Venice, that taste for paintings of familiar objects which it was customary to place in the

15

foreground of pictures and which other later artists made into still-lifes. We can thus see that the painters of the North had (should we say in their blood?) a greater familiarity with reality than the Italians. And although classifications of this nature should be taken with a grain of salt, it would seem that their approach was one of analysis rather than of synthesis. Together with Aertszen, that crude painter of peasants, we must also include among the precursors of this type of realism Marinus van Reymerswaele (1497–1570), a caricaturist of moneylenders and noted for his 'tooth extraction' pictures, Hans Sanders van Hemessen and Engelsbrechtszen, not to mention Quentin Matsys. But a painting cannot be explained only in terms of its theme and of the life of the society in which it is produced. The first works of the Dutch Realist school were portraits. It was only later in the century that the painters began to paint genre scenes, still-lifes, landscapes and animals. The early days of the Republic were translated in terms of the fine arts by an interminable gallery of usually not very flattering portraits. But there remains the question of where these portraits come from, of whence they derive their discretion, their contrasts of light and shade, their monochromatic icy quality, which is as glacial as the faces of the models who sat for them.

At that period Holland appears to be the central core of resistance to the international current of the Baroque, which had been born in Italy for the glory of the Counter-Reformation. This we can see in the great austerity of Dutch architecture, in the complete lack of theatricality in Dutch painting, the composition of which, although skilled enough, does not aim at virtuosity. But this opposition to the general trend does not mean that nothing found its way from Venice or Rome to the United Provinces. For, whilst the fashion for painters to make the Italian pilgrimage had passed, contacts at least remained numerous. We know that after 1566 painters such as Goltzius, Cornelius Cornelisz and Carel van Mander, continued to champion a mannerist style, derived directly from Italy, which they used in the painting of great mythological compositions. But their influence was waning. There are also references to the stay in Rome of three painters from Utrecht, a city more susceptible to

Roman influences than insular towns like Amsterdam. The three painters were van Baburen, Ter Brugghen and Gerhard Honthorst, known as 'Gherardo delle Notti,' who travelled to Rome at the beginning of the century to work either in Caravaggio's studio or with his pupils. Many varying conclusions have been drawn from these contacts between Utrecht and Rome, between Protestant and Papist. In particular it has been said that Rembrandt and Vermeer were, at a distance, pupils of Caravaggio. This would seem a somewhat rash conclusion. However, these Utrecht painters of the Roman school did inspire, in their own country, a natural tendency towards genre paintings and opposed the grave austerity of the portraits for which the taste had been developed by Protestantism.

We thus see what opposing currents were to clash in Holland at the beginning of the century: on the one hand, a national school of portrait painters drawing in a discreet manner, employing a sombre palette, careful to paint their sitters with the greatest possible accuracy, not attempting to flatter the outward man, but to give them that air of moral dignity which was their subjects' desire in real life. This school would rapidly get the better of the 'mannerist' painter with his surgical approach. And on the other hand, there would be a school with an alien tendency towards colour, which resurrected a national tendency towards genre scenes and invented figures in which the artists sought, above all, 'expression': a smile, a grimace, sadness.

The portrait, that foundation-stone of Dutch painting is, as we have already said, a national genre. In the 16th century, Jan van Scorel had already painted the twelve faces of the Catholic Knights of the Holy Land, and Dirk Barentsz and Cornelius Ketel, group portraits of Civil Guard Companies. Clearly they were not the only people in the world to paint gatherings of persons with faces framed by skilfully gauffered ruffs. But their models do not have the feverish expression of the rapt noblemen whom El Greco assembled in 1586 around the corpse of the Count d'Orgaz. Only Anthonis Moor of Utrecht, better known by the Spanish name of Antonio Moro, sometimes presented his models *en férocité*. There is, for instance, his portrait of the Duke of Alba, the 'pacifier' of the United

17

Provinces, which is equalled in severity only by Titian's Charles V. Moro became an international Court painter and attempted to show the gravity of his famous sitters. But the Dutch painters who never left their native land remain more intimate. Not so intimate, admittedly, as the Flemish painters, but they rarely abandon their natural good-humoured relationship with the person posing for them. True, they showed him in all his finery, but the black felt hat, the white collar and cuffs of the citizens are severe. And as for the officer at the head of his company, the painters permit themselves only the watered sheen of silk, a few lace frills and some plumes: a meagre feast for a colourist, but what a feast of grey for a Frans Hals! Gradually, we can see the emergence of that touch of humour which rescues the group portraits from the solemnity with which they were begun. Its growth is due to the painters' concern for realism, for they quickly found themselves faced with the problem of enlivening their collections of likenesses. To begin with they were content simply to line up faces; later they wished to show what had brought these men in uniform, these citizens, together and above all they wished to infuse life into that impossible subject – the group portrait.

We tire rather quickly of this succession of individual or group portraits. From picture to picture, we witness merely variations on the same theme. And it does not matter to us today whether we have before us the Archers of St Adrien or the officers of St George, the Governors of the St Elizabeth Almshouse or the Company of Captain Dirck Jacobsz. It is wrong, however, to dismiss these works painted to order too hastily. In them we can see how the artist and client collaborate, how the painter achieves greater and greater freedom from his subject.

In fact, at a time when religious art, freed at last from its duty of strict obedience to the 'rules' patiently set out by specialists, was beginning an independent career which would find its climax in the sumptuous apotheosis of a Tiepolo, painters in Holland were frequently subjected to the finnicking requirements of dozens of sitters imbued with their own importance, who quite naturally wished to be shown to the best advantage. We can easily imagine what discussions on the placing of the sitters must

have taken place, what arguments about precedence, and what advice on the 'good side' of a face must have preceded work on a picture – quite apart from the fact that the artist might have wished to add a figure turning his back or his head. But Rembrandt saw his popularity wane and his commissions become fewer after he dared to refuse to show the officers of Captain Frans Banning Cocq in the same field of light. And this although in the painting in question he raised the group portrait to a new level. For us, nothing shows more clearly than this picture what the regular rounds of the guard must have been like when the country was at war. We can readily understand, however, that the sitters were not very pleased to see their portrait pass into the shadow like that. Flattered though they might be at appearing in the centre of a brilliant and glorious scene, they had reason to doubt whether they could be recognised in this marching troop.

The group portrait, a typically Dutch genre, is thus the perfect example of 'directed' art, of utilitarian painting. Today we recognise both the convention and its limitations; but this dialogue between painter and sitter, often so close, so immediate, that it rarely produced the kind of portrait in which men of all periods wish to recognise themselves, nevertheless did not prevent one of the greatest painters of all times from fulfilling himself to order. Frans Hals apparently did not permit himself to deviate from the straight and narrow path. We know of only two rebellious, vengeful gestures – the two group portraits he painted in his old age of the male and female Governors of the Haarlem Almshouse, showing the former as drunkards and the latter as harpies. But his other portraits are not mere exercises in the classical manner; each of his canvasses becomes a marvellous, free invention, a game less tied to the contingent than many abstract paintings of today.

Such was the freedom which the painter gradually achieved in spite of the client – an astonishing freedom of execution which would lead him to paint the most extraordinary works while dealing with the most conventional subjects – an illicit freedom. Admittedly Frans Hals' successors were none too brilliant. It was his brush strokes they tried to imitate, his virtuosity and his range of greys which, for a time, was to divorce art

from colour. But Frans Hals remains inimitable; and if it was impossible to build on his work, he nevertheless formed or influenced many painters. For example Judith Leyster, who is almost a copyist, Adriaen Brouwer, Adriaen van Ostade and Jan Steen, would learn from him only verve and good humour, but they would become famous for their genre paintings, and their scenes of low life might have been painted by Frans Hals from anonymous models in an unrestrained moment.

For Frans Hals not only possesses an astonishing facility of brushwork; he brought the art of the group portrait to its peak of perfection. He was no doubt not the first to wish to break ranks, to wish to invest his assembled actors with animation and a semblance of action. Cornelis Cornelisz had carried out this little revolution before him, but Frans Hals began it anew, quite naturally; without any trace of effort, he sensed the vitality, the calm strength of these burghers who came to sit for him after returning from some tour of duty with the Civic Guard. The war against Spain had petered out in 1609, but there were still battles on the seas against the English and, later, on Dutch soil itself, against the armies of Turenne and Condé. The nation was therefore compelled to remain on guard and, at least in the early days of peace, the citizens were subjected to a strict observance of their military duties with the Civic Guard. Theirs was a modest war and certainly when Frans Hals undertook to paint their portraits, there was no real fighting. But they did not commission him to paint them in battle. These true realists did not ask the artist to invent. Anxious to have a good likeness, they posed at table, presenting themselves to posterity at the happy end of the banquet, which had been a tradition of their society since the Middle Ages. The dinner is almost at an end, but we do not find the archers gorging themselves joyfully. It is time for speeches and the Captain is explaining to his men that they have not gathered together to enjoy a good meal but to give proof of the noble sentiments which unite them. It is the moment of recollection and there is still something Calvinist and Republican in this naive desire to retain a certain degree of solemnity. Yet if we look closely at these burgomasters, these standard-bearers, they are all far gone in their cups. Some are close

to apoplexy. But they all keep their dignity. Meanwhile, only a few miles away from Amsterdam, Jordaens was painting people eating and drinking and making of it an occasion for unrestrained merriment, and Brouwer the Dutchman had only to instal himself in Catholic Antwerp to be free to paint good straightforward village orgies without having to concern himself, like his fellow-student, van Ostade, with illustrating some example of Republican virtue. There was, therefore, a natural censorship of the Arts, but it was light-handed. Frans Hals never came into collision with it; he lived freely within its rules, and these were not embarrassing to a painter who eschewed the nude. He carried out his rebellion, brush in hand, that brush with which he played as with a rapier, thrusting and cutting at light and form with the virtuosity of a fencer. He attained the peak of virtuosity in what we might call his 'genre portraits,' those faces of public house musicians and old witches, taken off at brush point. No doubt nowadays this 'genre' makes us feel slightly uncomfortable. We see in it mere facile picturesqueness, but with what zest Hals treats these subjects, and how well we can understand the enthusiasm of Manet! Perhaps we ought to see in the portrait of the 'Laughing Cavalier' more than the mere memory of friendships which the gay painter liked to strike up in the inns – perhaps a Roman influence imported by the Utrecht painters or an essay in the manner of that Dutch painter who became known to the Italians as Bamboccio. If it be true that Frans Hals is the painter of laughter, and that few artists have been able to vary as he did the expression on the faces of his group portraits, we must take particular note in these genre paintings of his extraordinary desire to enliven the faces, to catch them, as in a modern snapshot, with an expression which, although fugitive, reveals their feelings. Perhaps we can trace these feelings to the days of Caravaggio and the open-mouthed ballad singers of Ter Brugghen. Perhaps we should go back to the genre characters of Giorgione, to that *cantatore appassionato* in the Galleria Borghese which is now attributed to him, or even further back, to Leonardo da Vinci's studies in expression, or back to Breugel, who is closer to Frans Hals.

It seems more likely that in these few canvasses Hals wished to show his paces in a genre the fashion for which had been launched by the pupils of Caravaggio, when they reintroduced an already ancient tradition. But the charm of these genre paintings does not make us regret that Frans Hals pursued the career of official painter. He died poor and forgotten, but it he who has given us the most exact image of his country, of these good citizens who were the only ones in the world to make the dream of the Middle Ages a reality, with their republican, corporative society, a political anachronism which the French influence was to overthrow completely in the 18th century. For proof of this we need only look at the portrait by Frans Decker in the Haarlem Municipal Museum, which used to be the Almshouse. He painted it in 1737. It shows the successors of Frans Hals' Almshouse Governors. These Governors with their wigs and their languid expressions have nothing in common with the sitters whom Frans Hals, in his old age, had shown in their decline, but whom other pictures show in their vigour and health. The group portrait did not outlive the models of Frans Hals, that great painter of the greatest moment in Dutch history.

For it was only a moment. We are always reluctant to use the word 'decadence' because the history of art abounds in changes of opinion as to what constitutes decline or progress. Yet it seems clear that Dutch art became bastardised when the country, having become too prone to foreign influences, lost its political and moral individuality and that it reached its zenith between 1650 and 1660, that is to say during the moment of respite guaranteed by the Westphalian Peace Treaty. Ostade and Pieter de Hooch were to be succeeded by that excessively elegant painter, Cornelis Troost. The masters of the still-life such as Claesz and Heda, who had brought a marvellous simplicity to a pitch of perfection, were to be replaced by artists who painted more and more sumptuous subjects, which looked 'rich'. As for the landscape painters, they were to end up with conventional scenes. Dutch art was to be snuffed out until the French painters of the 19th century became enthusiastic over the masters of the Golden Age. It is then that they were to resurrect, in the good and bad senses of the word, what Van Gogh called, with an admiration he never lost, 'the old, undiluted Dutch style'.

This 'old Dutch style' was, as far as the pupils of Frans Hals were concerned, the genre painting; but it was also the still-life and the land-scape, that is to say, to put it simply and quote only the most famous names: Vermeer, Heda, Ruisdael. For Rembrandt is a miracle – the most Dutch of all Dutch painters no doubt, but one who more than any other oversteps the frontiers of his country. This 'old Dutch style,' as we have seen, was the sudden successor to the style of painting before the wave of iconoclasm. It was opposed not so much to the art of Lucas van Leyden or of Pieter Aertszen as to the mannered virtuosity of van Mander, Goltzius and Cornelis Cornelisz, compared with which it was marked by simplicity and sincerity, being a little priggish, slightly amusing but always of a great honesty. Van Gogh spoke of 'pure Dutch art': he was, we have seen, speaking of a tradition – a tradition of realism.

But is there, in effect, any great difference between a Breugel and a van Ostade? Undoubtedly all the difference between the genius and the minor painter, but van Ostade takes up once more the subjects dear to the Flemish painter. We may say that he paints scenes illustrating medieval proverbs; but they are no longer proverbial. If we look at the actors, they have not changed; they are still dressed in the same manner. There is, however, one difference in detail: van Ostade's peasants smoke. This was a fairly recent craze, which the painter wished to show, in a quite natural way, of course, and without the caricaturist's verve of a Brouwer who painted that snap-shot of a man smoking with mouth wide open to let the smoke escape. Van Ostade is the typical example of the Dutch painter working for a clearly defined clientèle, in a clearly defined genre, which he cultivates without being ordered to do so. Famous for his excellence in a well-circumscribed field, he produced peasant-scene after peasant-scene in both paintings and etchings. His works are very numerous, but this mass-producer maintained his quality. His painting even shows various trans-formations, proof that he avoided copying himself. Frans Hals taught him how to paint with the point of the brush: from Rembrandt he took his liking for subtle light effects, trembling in the shadows; and we follow with interest the evolution of a man who, as a good townsman, laughed discreetly at the country folk and liked their good-natured intimacy. If he never moves us, if the charm of his little stories generally escapes us, at least he holds our attention with his play of light on country-inn scenes in the open air, with his studies of peasant interiors in which we sometimes see him as a forerunner of Daumier. But he was and remains the most typical representative of that national school of painting which reacted against most foreign influences by showing only specialised subjects, treated in a particular way. His success, it must be added, was as great in Holland as it was abroad, if we are to judge by the number of pictures he painted and by the number of his works which, in the 18th century, were still the pride of the main Paris collections. His were certainly Dutch paintings, but his work was not unique, for Teniers and Brouwer in Antwerp were painting the gross peasant merrymaking with which we are all familiar, and at the same period Le Nain and Velasquez also depicted peasants. But the Spaniards and the French did so with an astonishing gravity, the Flemings with a ferocious zest which sometimes becomes disquieting, whereas the Dutch scenes, so minutely painted in all their details, aim only to amuse.

Adriaen van Ostade had made himself a rural specialist in genre painting; but many other painters in the same style would replace the cowherds by the actors in the thousand and one comedies of city life, painters like Ter Borch, Gerard Dou, Gabriel Matsu, Jan Steen, Hoghstraten, Brekelenkam, F. van Mieris, Caspar Netscher, Nicolas Maes, Pieter de Hooch and Vermeer. They were all very different, if not divergent artists who had been influenced by masters as far apart as Rembrandt and Frans Hals; yet they were all united in the same cult of the Dutch scene. Among them there are colourists and devotees of the chiaroscuro. Some take pleasure in staging a picture as an author composes a scene of a play. Others are interested only in the interplay of light and colour; but all introduce us into Dutch middle-class homes, into houses washed and shiny as new pins and to domestic security.

At a time when Dutch sailors were sailing between Curaçao and China as if they were on their native seas, or daily facing Norwegian ice, when

24

every port was introducing new customs to the nation, the only subject which interested painters and art lovers alike was a nice Dutch scene. If ever there were travellers who closed their eyes to the exotic, it was surely the merchants of the United Provinces. On their walls they wished to see their serving girls, their glass, their silver, their furniture, their animals, their little houses. It is as if Holland and the Dutch way of life were paradise enough, as if they were sufficiently wise to be of the opinion that we can know the world just as well by keeping ourselves to our own street or our own drawing room as by sailing the Seven Seas. They were Dutch through and through, even down to their pictures, and their Holland is a country of the little incidents of a tranquil life, untroubled by any metaphysical doubts or carnal passion. The days of the Revolution and of Protestantism, of the struggle against the occupying power, when life was governed by principles drawn from the Bible, are gone for ever. The worthy civic guards and the governors, busy with their deeds of charity, are replaced by a smug, fashionable banking middle-class – a middle-class imbued with its own importance, and the importance of the little rites which seem to suffice it as a raison d'être. A century later, Pietro Longhi, Francesco Guardi and Tiepolo would produce the same paintings of mœurs but in different colours. We tire rather quickly of this art which is devoted to the admiration of a civilisation that is either domestic or worldly. But in these pictures we must look beyond the subjects they represent, even when they do it with the blatancy which marks the raconteur. According to Marcel Proust, the writer Bergotte offered his entire works for the little patch of yellow wall in Vermeer's 'View of Delft'. Walls of such quality are rare in painters like Steen and Matsu, Ter Borch or Gerard Dou. However, this is precisely what we seek in painting today. Compared to Ostade, Rembrandt seems a foreigner. Perhaps to some extent he continues that pro-Roman school against which the new Dutch realist art rebelled. When the majority of painters had launched into an extreme realism, he formed with his pupils a reactionary pocket of resistance and aimed to show that art is not only landscape, portrait, an examination of nature rather than a mode of self-expression, but that it can also be composition, invention,

25

the expression of a drama, the translation of a mystery. Rembrandt was to lead the opposition to the general tendency of his contemporaries. There is general agreement that he came under Italian influence through the works of the Pyras brothers and the advice of his mentors, Jacob van Swanenburgh and Pieter Lastman, who had been the pupils of Adam Elsheimer in Italy. Very little is actually known about Elsheimer, a German resident in Rome, the author of small, very carefully painted landscapes and compositions on Biblical subjects, which are treated with a naturalness contrary to the prevalent decadent mannerist style. His works are still frequently mistaken for those of Saraceni and Leclerc. But we are not at all certain that he was one of the painters who came under Caravaggio's influence. More than one art historian contests this point, assuring us that Elsheimer did not acquire his predilection for the chiaroscuro from Caravaggio, but from a tradition which goes back to Bassano. However, whether it was Pieter Lastman or the writings of Carel van Mander, an admirer of Caravaggio, who initiated the trend, Rembrandt paid homage to the 'caravaggesque' fashion of chiaroscuro and violent composition, with its large planes and a play of light which transforms shapes to the point where they acquire new meaning.

This influence is not very marked in Rembrandt's earlier works. 'St Paul in Prison' and 'Tobias and Sarah', both painted before the age of twenty-one, in the studio which, after only six months' study with Lastman, he shared with his fellow pupil Jan Lievens, are in fact good, rather heavy paintings, with a healthy, clear light, solid but without any stylistic affectation. He even took pains to slip in such details as the little dog, the string of onions hanging from a nail, the bird cage, which clearly bear the Dutch hallmark.

Towards 1628 (Rembrandt was then twenty-two) there emerges his desire for expression (we might almost say for 'expressionism'): here we find gestures of terror, staring eyes, ghostly figures, highly effective contrasts of light and shadow, extremely realistical passages set against completely fantastic backgrounds. It is great tragic drama such as had not been played since Shakespeare and the Elizabethans, a drama of contrasts which we rediscovered only with the Romantics and the spotlight. Was this Caravaggio's influence? Today, as we have seen, we are assured that we ought to credit Bassano with the invention of this game of light and shade. No doubt this makes it easier to understand the various aesthetic movements which succeeded each other in Europe in the 16th century; but neither Caravaggio nor Bassano explains Rembrandt. Lastman doubtless makes the transition easier, but if we find in Rembrandt more than one light effect, which we have already noted in the vast architectural paintings of Saraceni or Leclerc where a few trembling rays of light pick out scattered groups engaged in mysterious tasks, there is nothing in common between the sensual realism of Caravaggio, transfigured as it is by light and shade, and the more subdued effects which the Dutch master employs to set a less turbulent scene. In fact, Rembrandt does not need the whole gamut of spotlights, nor complicated machinery, to obtain special effects. He does not seek unusual gestures or unexpected, twisted shapes; light, in his case, aims at something more than producing the mere shape of a body, something more than what is required for a lyrical composition. It is diffused throughout the painting; it is born in it, it palpitates in the shadow; it is most often the real object of the canvas, a streak of daylight vibrating in the falling night.

Nevertheless, the Italian influence is apparent in more than one trait shared by both schools. It marked Rembrandt for life. Not that he was always to remain faithful to these effects of chiaroscuro; it is debatable which of his paintings are the finest, his portraits in the classical Dutch manner, like the 'Syndics of the Cloth Hall' or the 'Anatomy Lesson', group portraits renewing the good old tradition, or works like the 'Jewish Bride,' full of mysterious brilliance, strange lights and shades. But this italianate style, which makes such a successful contrast with solid Protestant realism, we find once more in Rembrandt's habit of composing allegorical figures, in the pleasure he found in painting Saskia, and later Hendrickje Stoffels, as Flora. In this connection, we are constantly reminded that, no doubt for only a short period, he studied at the University of Leyden, where several teachers taught the science of emblems.

We also find foreign influences in a genre which is rare in Holland but which Rembrandt would nevertheless attempt: the nude. It would appear that for Rembrandt nudity was only, as Valéry has said: 'Le temps d'un sein nu entre deux chemises'; in love with Saskia and later with Hendrickje, he painted them only in the intimacy of the bed chamber. His nudes are the secret visions of a man who does not idealise feminine beauty, either in terms of that opulence dear to Rubens, or of that elegance which Botticelli loved; they are the visions of a man who paints the nude with an astonishing care for truth and a passion which, although controlled, is none the less striking. Finally, in his unceasing concern for expression, in his passion for painting himself smiling, gloomy or in desperate mood, in showing in fact all the grimaces of life, he goes back not only to Frans Hals, who was obsessed by the expression of laughter, but back also to that Italian fashion, which can perhaps be traced to da Vinci, of painting 'faces in action', of achieving a snapshot effect.

Whatever may have been the bonds of parentage between his art and that of the Italian painters, Rembrandt renewed the national genres, the portrait and the group portrait. We have merely to look at what he made, when twenty-six years old, of 'Professor Nicolaes Pietersz. Tulp's Anatomy Lesson', to see what he does at the age of thirty-six with the 'Night Watch' and at fifty-six with the 'Syndics of the Cloth Hall'. There can be no doubt that, in these three compositions, we witness a clearcut evolution towards simplicity, for the latter is one of the most austere, and one of the richest, of Dutch paintings; but we can also see how this painter who seemed the most susceptible of all to foreign influences, remains, in the last resort, a great master of Dutch realist art. Henri Matisse has said: 'We only know one saying of Rembrandt: "I paint portraits" and in the storm I have often clung to these words.'

In Rembrandt's life there was a period of opulence. It opens with the commissioning, by the Amsterdam Surgeons' Guild, of the group portrait of its principal members assembled around Professor Tulp. What a compliment to the newly-found fame of a painter who had been living in the city for only a year. From then on Rembrandt had a fashionable career before him; he was to become a portrait painter who strove to satisfy his clients by describing them with the accuracy they demanded. But on the whole his best portraits would be those he painted from anonymous models whom he dressed to his liking and not those inspired by the rich middle-class citizens of Amsterdam who came knocking at his door in their finery. Very soon in such canvasses as his 'Judas' (1629), which so struck one of the painter's first visitors, Constantin Huygens, he would return to the fantastic world he discovered at Leyden, the biblical world with its strange costumes, the gleam of arms, its gold embroidered cloth and carpets. We have said that the Dutch did not understand the exotic; to say that is to exclude Rembrandt. But his Orient is in fact no more accurate than that of Carpaccio or Piero della Francesca. At first, he limits himself to a few turbans and various accessories, but soon, to make us believe that the personages of the Old Testament or the Passion live again before our eyes, he will require only a little light, shining on some precious stuffs, on armour or on musical instruments. Rembrandt had the Orient under his own roof in the shape of the antiques he bought with the passion of a second-hand dealer, together with pictures, drawings and etchings. They lend his can-vasses something of the magic dusty quality of the bazaars as one imagines them in Jerusalem, sacred bazaars almost, in which each object seems to have a fabulous past and disposes man to meditation and even to prayer.

'Here are my antiques,' he used to say, pointing to his helmets, his furs, his carpets. And if his paintings did not suffice to make him understood, we can guess from these few words in what a solitary position Rembrandt was gradually going to find himself, divorced from strictly Protestant painting, divorced from those artists who could continue religiously to venerate Greek marbles and Roman bronzes. Finally, the naturalism at which Rembrandt aimed (and, amongst others, a work like the self-portrait in Dresden shows what he strove for) put him in opposition to the genre painters and the painters of interiors who merely rung the changes on well established themes.

Rembrandt had numerous pupils, however: Carel Fabritius, Jan Victors, Nicolas Maes, Aert de Gelder, Gerbrandt van den Eeckhout, Ferdinand Bol and Govaert Flinck, were among those who listened to his teaching, some at the peak of his fame, when his studio was divided into cells where each worked peacefully, some like Aert de Gelder, when Rembrandt saw the masters of the Amsterdam Town Hall refuse the picture they had commissioned from him ('The Conspiracy of Claudius Civilis', which is now in the Stockholm Museum).

But in the last resort, Rembrandt's teaching left them all bewildered; the personality of the master was so strong that they were obliged to submit to it entirely. And to find themselves again, they had to deny his teaching. If Bol, Flinck and Fabritius occupy an important place in 17th-century Dutch art, it is because they fell back into line and painted peaceful interiors, genre scenes and portraits of Almshouse Governors. Aert de Gelder, on the other hand, continued to follow Rembrandt in his subjects and in his technique. Clearly he was not alone in continuing to paint historic subjects and the studio of Pieter Lastman must have had more than one offshoot in the country. Nevertheless, it is clear that the last glimmerings of the spirit of his master were snuffed out completely with de Gelder. In fact it is tempting to see in Rembrandt's miserable end, albeit an end brightened by unique discoveries, the symbol of the death of a concept. There is in his last paintings a serene melancholy which reminds us of the pure expressions of a Leonardo da Vinci, of a Dürer, a Goya or an El Greco, expressions which did not evoke an echo in their own time because to hear them one must belong to a different age.

The proof is that at the very moment when the public of Leyden and thereafter the whole of Holland, whom Europe would follow in their enthusiasm, had eyes only for Gerard Dou, Rembrandt ceased to please them by plunging into original research. Yet Gerard Dou came to Leyden to learn the rudiments from Rembrandt, his elder by seven years, and under his direction to paint the portraits of his patron and of his relatives, those patient models for the new studio. But Rembrandt had hardly gone to Amsterdam when Dou renounced history and its pomp and set himself up as a genre painter. He painted, with a minute attention to detail which made him famous, scenes in which the semi-darkness which surrounded

Rembrandt's mysteries was used merely to give a certain distinction to a dropsical woman, to a woman plucking hens, to a fishwife and to any number of young girls at their windows, small pictures which people kept carefully in precious wooden boxes. Dou is a sleek van Ostade. His pupils and imitators, Metsu, Netscher, and van Mieris, added refinements to the little scenes of comedy which he stages in each of his paintings.

Gerard Dou was able not only to satisfy but to fill with enthusiasm those people who seek in painting only fidelity, minute exactness of detail and malicious observation. Europe fought over his pictures. It is only sixty years ago since the 'Dropsical Woman' was still hung in the place of honour in that holy of holies, the *Salon Carré* of the Louvre. Present-day taste has lowered Gerard Dou's standing; but whatever value is still attributed to him, this painter could not fail to be over-estimated. Dutch painting was to die because of this over-estimation, not of an excess of realism, but because it confounded realism and convention.

Does that mean that genre painting had no followers after the refined painting of Gerard Dou, van Ostade, Metsu, Ter Borch and Jan Steen, and could only consolidate established positions? Undoubtedly many painters held that view, and since the market for the genre scene or the painting of mœurs was the most flourishing, next to that for the portrait, and well ahead of the demand for seascapes and still-lifes, they launched into it and were able to apply reasonably subtle gifts to carve out for themselves a place in the history of Dutch art. And this, not only in spite of the great abundance of painters in those days but in spite, too, of the incredible number of pictures which at that time decorated every home, wealthy or modest.

However, other artists showed that the genre could be given new life. One of them, Pieter de Hooch, has remained almost as famous as he was in his lifetime. The fame of the other, who died at the age of forty-three, underwent a complete eclipse in the 18th century, and it is only in the last hundred years that we have become interested in him, so interested, indeed, that we consider him one of the greatest painters of the Low Countries and are reluctant to put him on the same footing with other painters of interiors; yet they were his peers. We know of only some forty pictures by Jan Vermeer van Delft, but they suffice to make him Rembrandt's equal.

He has been defined as a painter of still-lifes and it is true that he was not much concerned with faces and their expressions. He looks at them with the same curiosity as he does at a breadcrumb or a stone jar. And yet his contemporaries saw him, like Pieter de Hooch or Emmanuel de Witte, as a painter of interiors.

Gerard Dou and van Ostade are worlds apart from Ter Borch, Metsu or Caspar Netscher. One is a world where people are amused by buffoons and peasants; the other, the world of a more refined caste, wishes to see in its pictures the reflection of its own wealth and good breeding. There are also signs of an evolution towards less heavy tones in painting. It was about the middle of the century when, perhaps under the influence of the landscape painters and the painters of animals in the open air, painting was enriched by a light which no longer came from a narrow window or a lamp carried through the night, but had all the brilliance of the sun. Looking at the early canvasses of Rembrandt and the light ones of Vermeer, people have been able to say, putting it simply, that each of them, in his own exceptional and original way, represented the two aspects of the school of Caravaggio and Caravaggesque taste; the one dark, the other light, one nocturnal, the other seeking the broad light of day. This view is now disputed and people refuse to credit Caravaggio with having inspired the light tones of the Utrecht painters, Ter Brugghen, Honthorst and van Baburen. But that does not really matter because there are in the works of these painters many signs of a certain direct descent from the art of Caravaggio, if only in the somewhat low expression of the characters depicted, who are often far gone in drink; moreover it is clear that, after their return from Italy, these travelled painters merely revived a trend which was very natural in a country under the tight rein of Protestantism— the tendency to paint 'fast life'.

Before he adhered to the Dutch tradition, Vermeer himself paid his homage to mythological, allegorical or bacchic compositions imported from

Italy. Thus, one of the first works attributed to him is Diana surrounded by her nymphs, now at the Mauritshuis in the Hague, and the 'Procuress' in the Dresden Museum, a very correct scene, but one nevertheless which is the prologue to an orgy. It is therefore no surprise to find that in 'The Studio' (about 1665), now in Vienna, Vermeer shows his model posing for an allegorical figure, crowned with laurels, with a book under one arm and a Roman trumpet under the other. There is also the problem of the religious paintings Vermeer painted in his youth. The quarrels that the case of the forger van Meegeren stirred up round the 'Last Supper' and 'The Pilgrims to Emmaus' which are, after all, simply bad paintings, are still fresh in our memories. One has to be a very great Vermeer expert to discover in them the imprint of the master of the 'Astronomer,' 'The Studio,' 'The Woman in the Red Hat' or, to confine ourselves to early works, the characteristics of the painter of 'Jesus in the House of Martha and Mary.' But what is important here, is to see that Vermeer, like Rembrandt, was to begin with much more open to international artistic currents than to the strict rules of national painting.

But, whilst Gerard Dou was selling his pictures for between eight hundred and one thousand florins, Vermeer, whose 'Little Street' (now at the Amsterdam Museum) only after his death found a buyer for seventy-two florins, was revolutionising painting and raising Dutch genre painting to its highest peaks. We have seen how, with Ter Borch, the originally rather crude genre of the early peasant scenes had softened to show the urbanity and quiet of middle-class interiors, how the soldiers no longer hold the servant girl so tight but have learnt to pay a respectful court to the young ladies they have come to visit. Simultaneously the lighting becomes more subtle. And painters of interiors came to the fore who were working with a lighter range of colours, men like Pieter de Hooch and Emmanuel de Witte, who drew their inspiration from church painters like Pieter Saenredam (whose simplicity is particularly congenial to present day sensibility) and cultivated in their turn the pretty vistas of forms set in perspective in order to show the luminous calm of the little houses of the United Provinces. Vermeer was to take this study of light to its ultimate conclusions, but before him Pieter de Hooch (at least during his stay at Leyden, since later, in Amsterdam, he was compelled to enliven his pictures with little comedies of Dutch life) had expressed the happy peace of a sunlit house. The interplay of tiled floors, vistas of corridors, supplemented by the perspective of the pictures on the walls – these are the innumerable, almost abstract elements which the painter manipulates with that meticulous geometrical precision which modern critics find in a contemporary Dutchman, the austere Piet Mondrian. The geometry is more subtle and complicated in the works of Vermeer, who devoted himself, like Cézanne, to a scientific study of volume in space. The painters of Delft thus arrived at paintings of interiors in which the human presence is very discreet. Either, as is frequently the case, the model turns his back to the painter, or the face is shown against the light. Then we find a meticulous game of forms and colours; the canvas is, as it were, divided into geometrical surfaces, the perfection of which is brought out by the minuteness with which certain realistic details are painted – such details, for example, as door keys or the bristles of a broom. The picture has at one and the same time some of the quality of a *trompe l'œil* and of an architectural drawing; the strangeness of the one and the severity of the other, being in strong contrast, trap the observer into dreaming in an extraordinary manner. How far we are here from the little anecdotes of Steen, Ter Borch and van Ostade! The anecdote escapes the painter, and he is compelled to use all the resources of his art to continue to surprise the viewer, who is clearly disconcerted by the change. This painting in multiple perspective is of a high virtuosity: the doors are always open to show other rooms, then the courtyard and sometimes the garden or the house opposite. The painter multiplies the variations of the tiled floors at will. There is a landscape there which, as it were, pierces the wall on which it is hung, and we can distinguish some framed study of a musical instrument, seen in a foreshortened perspective. To these *haute école* exercises are added the subtle transparencies of light, which comes sometimes through double or single framed windows, sometimes through a curtain, and the effects of shadows on the ground. There is, in this sphere, no more remarkable work than the picture in the Louvre attributed to the school of Vermeer, the sole subject of which is three communicating rooms. This picture has been called 'The Slippers' because of the pair of slippers in the central room, which appears to be a passage. In the foreground, against the light, there is the handle of the open door, which we see only as a vertical green line; then, leading the eye towards the wall of the third room, a bunch of keys hanging on the third door. We never tire either of the meticulous game, or of the prodigy of fidelity. We can go as far as to say that, with this scientific geometry in space, the painters of Delft succeeded in giving a new lease of life to that realism which is indispensable if one wishes to please the Dutch. But, handled in this manner, incorporated into such an intellectual construction, it acquires quite another flavour. And where the descendants of Dou or Ter Borch found only triteness, the virtuosi of Delft were able to discover a new type of expression.

We can thus see the reasons for the enthusiasm of modern painters for these Dutch interiors—namely the science of geometrical composition and a certain daring in the way objects are placed in the foreground in order to accentuate the impression of depth. Vermeer remains the most daring in this field, while de Witte and de Hooch seem more timid; they do not understand such complicated compositions as when Vermeer put in the foreground of 'The Love Letter' in the Amsterdam Museum two dark planes, the panel of the door and a leather chair laden with numerous objects set against a wall; between these two dark surfaces there streams out, as if we had surprised it through the half-open door, the real subject of the picture: a patch of light which takes shape as two women, a musical instrument and a broom on the inevitable tiled floor. Again, in the foreground of the 'Sleeper' in the New York Metropolitan Museum, there is a chair outlined as if by some Japanese etcher or, to come nearer home, a Vuillard. The careful viewer could find material here for hours of dreams: the science of painting exploits every trick in its repertoire to hold the attention of the collector of anecdotes.

Yet there is more to Vermeer than this quasi-scientific mastery of the *trompe l'œil* and geometry. He is the master of another, uncodified science which, in his time, he was the only one to care for or to know about: the science of light. Today the simple words 'When light becomes colour' can arouse passion in most artists. In fact, they seek the same pictorial and intellectual alchemy as Vermeer discovered, the alchemy which distinguishes him from other painters in the intimate manner. True, his daring formal construction, which brings him close to Cézanne (for he creates space through his surface modulations), his freedom of composition, and the vigour with which he arranges his planes, would be sufficient to distinguish him. But he is also unique, as we can see particularly clearly in 'The Milkmaid,' in his manner of painting with little dots which are like brilliant pearls that catch the light from outside the local colour and give a luminous texture to the canvas. Then he abandons himself to a kind of counterpoint between form, colour, light and composition, to a hundred-voiced fugue, a patient labour which does not cause him to lose any of his spontaneity or ease. The effects of perspective achieved by Pieter de Hooch are sometimes a little forced, but the prodigious amount of work which Vermeer put into each of his canvasses does not in any way affect their suppleness. He evokes calm, silence and happiness with apparently as much facility as the most deft of landscape painters. But the impressions which he imparts to us are not fugitive. They have a gravity that fixes them for ever in our memory. It is a perfectly balanced art without brutal effects. Vermeer would seem to be unique in the history of art, did we not find in Chardin, in Corot and in Cézanne something of the same perfection. And we can well understand that every historian who has dealt with Vermeer, has tried, like Malraux, to reduce still further the already small number of paintings which can be attributed to him: it is only in master-pieces that his touch is to be seen.

Was Vermeer a still-life painter? Yes, if the art of the still-life is the game man plays with the forms of nature. But all the Dutch painters of the so-called minor genre did not have his synthetic vision, which is so uncommon in that analytical country. Nevertheless, it is perhaps owing to Vermeer's success that we take the painters of the 'Silent Life' more seriously today.

36

In Holland, the sources of this style of painting are twofold. On the one hand, artists such as Weenix, Melchior d'Hondekoeter or the brothers Marcellis tend to strike us rather as naturalists, botanists or entomologists. Their canvasses are sought after because of the exactness with which they depict dead animals or varieties of rare flowers. On the other hand, the Dutch have remained faithful to the medieval tradition of painting symbolic objects. Hence the skull we find placed on a book, a theme taken from the 'Vanity' dear to Holbein and Dürer. But the originality of the Dutch consists in having considered the inanimate object much more simply; good realists as they were, they were the first to christen this as yet ill-defined genre 'still-leven,' *immobile life*, or better still, *immobile model*. At last they had found a model which does not move and which can be analysed calmly and at leisure. Hence innumerable canvasses intended to display, as one displays in a showcase an insect or a butterfly, the curious, precious object which might interest the amateur; for the amateur who possesses a collection of curiosities naturally flatters himself that he knows something of science and wants an instructive picture. This was a field which might have been merely descriptive, a continuation of the inventory-like still-lifes of the previous century, one in which the artists could have exploited only the delicacy of their brushwork; but in fact it was in this field that the Dutch artists gave proof of the poetic spirit which they so often lacked in other subjects. For the still-life underwent more or less the same variations, the same evolution as the so-called major genres. Caravaggio created a sensation. The nocturnal still-life was introduced and, in Holland, the still-life was adapted to the different evolution of Dutch society. Austerity, morality and richness succeeded each other from the brush of Willem Kalf, van Beyeren and Davidsz. de Heem. But it should be stressed that gradually the painters paid less attention to description than to atmosphere and that they began to study light with as much attention as the glass on which it plays. Admittedly, this was to become a formula with Jan van Huysum, who excels in rendering the lustre of a grape, the gleam of a flower petal and the tenseness of the vine tendrils over which the butterfly dances in flight. Is that too clever? No doubt, but we accept such skill more easily in the still-life than in any other genre; for, after all, the still-life aims only at decoration.

Yet the painters of 'still-leven' of the Golden Age as a whole contributed a great deal to the still-life. The fact that, as good realists and analysts, they introduced some order into the genre, clearly did not make for originality of expression. Flower painters did not paint silver-ware; silver-ware painters were distinct from those who painted laid tables or the others who depicted bric-à-brac, from the bird painters or the painters of insects or the painters of reptiles. Each marked out for himself a clearly defined field.

Nevertheless, van Steck, Heda, Davidsz. de Heem and Pieter Claesz (who sometimes has a touch of Vermeer), together with numerous other artists, were able to give the still-life its patent of nobility and to make of an *ontbijtje* (that is to say, to make of the plates, glasses and dishes found on the traditional Dutch breakfast-table) more than just a picture to whet the appetite. Clearly all these painters played up to the national taste for precision and exactness by their admirable handling of the way light is reflected in a silver cup; sometimes, in order to astonish the spectator, they even amused themselves by smuggling the painter's silhouette into the reflection of a window on a goblet of Murano glass. But sooner or later we tire of the refinement of their brushwork which, like a botanical slide under the microscope, shows us the grain of a piece of lemon peel; we feel we want to follow the dialogue of form and colour beyond and get away from herring, oysters, fruit and biscuits. When they do break away we often find more humanity in these painters' *ontbijtjes* than in their portraits. Cézanne reminded us of this truth fifty years ago. Our search for it is not yet at an end.

All honour to the Dutch painters for having understood this. Whether, like Heda and Claesz, they were concerned to be discreet and chose only simple subjects, which they treated more in terms of tone values than of colour, or whether like Willem Kalf, Abraham van Beyeren and Jan Davidsz. de Heem they painted sumptuous works in which Ming bowls are found side by side with German 16th-century gold and silver ware and so transformed the still-life into an antique dealer's showcase, all of them knew how to express through these objects what it was generally held could be expressed only in compositions of the noble genre. The still-life painters, through their concern for 'speaking' composition, prepared the way for Vermeer whose work may be said to crown and epitomise Dutch national art. However, in their studies of light, the landscape painters too foreshadowed his style of painting.

If we say 'the Dutch landscape', two images immediately appear before our eyes: skaters on ice and cows in a meadow by the waterside. We do not need to look at them more closely to know that they are not both by the same artist. In this field, too, although not quite to the same degree as with the still-life artists, each painter has his speciality, church interiors, the countryside, the sea, the countryside with cows, townscapes, etc. This is yet another proof of the all-pervading Dutch orderliness. The general evolution of the Dutch landscape conforms to that of the other genres.

The origins of the landscape lie in scenes of the Dutch at work and play: above all at play, for Dutch painting did not attempt to show work except for picturesque effects, which already smack of tourism and folklore. Dutch painting aims to please, to distract, and the spectacle of work is therefore inopportune. So we have, in a less serious vein but still in the manner of Breugel, who was not Dutch, it is true, but who nevertheless is behind painting of this kind, a whole collection of Sundays on the frozen canals. Averkamp, for his part, continues the tradition of the medieval miniaturists, who liked to paint the seasons and the way in which they regulate the life of men; but this is not the only medieval source of the Dutch landscape. The tradition that the landscape must be a microcosm, that it must reassemble, from a point of vantage, mountains, valleys, plains, rivers, towns and, in the distance, lakes if not the sea, remains firmly implanted. In this case the landscape is a work composed in the studio, a work in which the artists sometimes use details painted from life. And how moving they are, these patches of local colour in certain German or Flemish masters when they appear in a sumptuous décor which claims to represent a vision of the whole world!

On the other hand, we note more than one trait common to these artificial productions and the landscapes which the Dutch painter sought in Italy. Lake Trasimeno or the Tivoli cascades are strange spectacles for the inhabitants of a flat country; and Breenbergh, van Poelenburgh, Both, Berchem and Hackaert who, at various times made the journey to Italy, had learnt to compose in a manner which did not differ greatly from that of the universal landscapists. In both cases, their pictures are constructed according to quasi-architectural rules. Generally the artist could not dispense with human figures who are there to tell a story which may be biblical, mythological or merely bucolic in the Dutch style. Claude Lorrain would require some Greek pretext for his landscapes; a Dutchman, were he Romanist or not, would import foreign pastures and in them place the cows, peasants and skaters of his own country.

We thus find the point of departure for Dutch landscape painting in the familiar figures of Averkamp, Arent Arentsz, Esaias and Jan van de Velde, Willem Buytewech and Visscher, the etcher and draughtsman, who is perhaps the true inventor of this genre in Holland. All these painters took part in the same movement of reaction against the contrived art of van Mander and Goltzius as Frans Hals or Adriaen van Ostade. Their drawing would be realistic; their aim, naturalness; and their common danger, that not all of them would eschew the anecdote. With them, unlike van Poelenburgh, the setting remains typically Dutch. At the very moment when the still-life painters renounced painting complete meals and contented themselves with a few glasses or plates, the landscape painters would reduce the importance of the human figure and paint only an avenue of trees or a thicket by the waterside. The same evolution occurred in the seascape. Painters began with real portraits of ships; then they showed historic battles, finally they sought only to show ships in the light that lies over the sea. This turning point came around 1630, but it was not the work of new painters. We can see it beginning in some of the masters who produced the first flowering of the art of the landscape, men like Pieter Molijn, Aert van der Neer, Salomon van Ruysdael and Jan van Goyen.

Even before Ruisdael thought of it, Van Goyen puts us in mind of the light playing on the water of the canals and in the mists rising from the sea. There is a town in the distance, some boats, sometimes a cow or a tree in the foreground, an occasional unevenness of the ground; but the real subject of the picture lies in the dialogue between the sky and the Dutch plain, which disappears into infinity, dappled with shadows cast by the moving clouds. Cuyp and Van Goyen are painters of the earth; Willem van de Velde, Porcellis, Van Everdingen are painters of the sea, but, in their best pictures, all will paint only the sky. This they will do with more or less subtleness, according to their talent, but all, on the whole, in a happy mood, an expression of their 'joie de vivre', that same satisfaction at being Dutch as both Van Ostade and Frans Hals showed in their works.

This splendidly tidy arrangement has its exceptions: they are Savery, Seghers, Rembrandt and Ruisdael. Admittedly, we find in Ruisdael's panoramas the same joy as Cuyp or Koninck express, but Ruisdael painted (and this had not been done before) the deserted countryside, the drama of the twisted shape of an oak. In his etchings and in his paintings, he used violent contrasts of light and dark which enabled him to interpret the most intense emotions. He demonstrated, finally, to those men who had won their land from the sea and wished it to be peaceful and disciplined that nature is disquieting. Had he really seen such tragic trees and bushes? There was something of a visionary in Ruisdael, as in Savery, in Seghers and Rembrandt.

Savery and Seghers still belong to the 16th century. This is no doubt the reason why we feel them to be closer to us than Hobbema, the elegant disciple of Ruisdael. Savery peopled disquieting forests, which Altdorfer would have loved, with animals from Noah's Ark, but he holds our attention above all by the wash drawings he made in the Tyrol, which are a good expression of his emotion when faced with the chaotic disorder of the mountains. In Seghers' deserted panoramas we sense that his vision is at one with the philosophy of those artists who, two hundred years earlier, wished to paint the earth in the same way as they painted man. Rembrandt admired Seghers' art to the point of acquiring eleven of his pictures. He introduced some Dutch highlights by his unconventional manner of treating terrain and light. But he did this whilst still remaining unmatched, even in a picture like the one now in the Cassel Museum, in which, in his turn, he tackles a skating scene. In Jacob Ruisdael, whose genius remains purely Dutch, and characteristic of his period, we find, in fact, the true Dutch landscape, a landscape with neither the Italian sense of the dramatic nor the desire, which still survived, to transform landscape into a microcosm.

Ruisdael lived and died poor, poor like Frans Hals and Rembrandt, forgotten in his life as was Vermeer after his death. In the fate of these men we see reflected the originality, the limitations and the highlights of the Dutch school of the Golden Century. The background from which these four exceptional personalities emerge is of a prodigious richness. The United Provinces, a small nation, had more painters than France or Germany, and their vast number was not made up of negligible artists, for it was they who introduced such new genres as the group portrait and developed the still-life and the landscape in a truly revolutionary manner. They give perfect proof of the balance which their society was seeking. Of the wars which it had to fight they give a much less clear picture but they are in harmony with their times, their social background, their status and, finally, in spite of the influences which contrived to affect them, they live in almost complete autonomy. Yet the lustre of their school was to fade at the end of the century, perhaps because they had too long lived self-contained lives and were incapable of change. The public would demand novelties, including French ones, to which they would be unable to adapt their temperaments.

Such general characteristics would in themselves constitute the glory of the Golden Century. But the contempt in which the most remarkable personalities of this school sooner or later came to be held shows the limitations of this excessively national art. Hals was more or less abandoned because of the increasing freedom with which he painted and because of his vigorous touch, to which people preferred expertly polished paintings. Rembrandt saw himself forgotten because he had launched out into the composition of biblical subjects, a genre which no longer interested many people, and in which he revealed himself in a disconcerting manner. Ruisdael lived modestly because he introduced drama into subjects where the public sought merely the pleasure of a simple country walk. Lastly, Vermeer introduced too much limpidness, simplicity and mystery into compositions where people would have preferred to find a story.

Dutch art, whose place in society was much the same as that of art today, underwent pressure from its public which led it irresistibly to the anecdote, to an exactness which anticipated the photograph and to facile poetry. That is how its admirers wanted it and we, in our turn, often find it admirable. This question remains: how can we find words to describe this century of Dutch painting which includes painters whose work is timeless, painters like Rembrandt, Frans Hals, Ruisdael and Vermeer?

# BIOGRAPHICAL NOTES

### HENDRICK AVERKAMP – 1585–1634

Born at Amsterdam, died at Kampen. His teacher, Gillis van Coninxloo, made him grasp the lessons of Breugel, but he was able to free himself from this influence and to pave the way, in winter scenes of great delicacy, for the purely Dutch landscapists.

### ARAHAM VAN BEYEREN – 1620/1621?–1690

Born at The Hague, died at Overschie. Pupil of Pieter Potter. A still-life painter, he worked in the principal towns of the Netherlands. The refinement of the objects he displays makes him almost a dealer in antiques. He seeks the rare piece and composes sumptuous works which are perhaps a little overloaded, but are held together by his exceptional sense of colour and harmony.

### AELBERT CUYP – 1620–1691

Born and died at Dordrecht. He was his father's pupil, but it was Jan van Goyen tho influenced his first steps and led him gradually to paint, using only a restricted range of colours, the subtle transparency of the Dutch sky. But the sun-drenched Italian landscape attracted him and he made concessions to the fashion imported from Rome by the Utrecht painters, in particular by Jan Both. However, he was able to integrate this Italianate style with the Dutch background and to paint in an original manner the men, animals and meadows of his country lit by the strange light of sunrise and sunset.

### GERARD DOU – 1613–1675

Born in Leyden. His father was a glass blower and glass etcher, who had him taught drawing and etching by two masters before sending him to Rembrandt's studio at the age of fifteen. He worked from nature and his principal models were Harmen and Neeltge, Rembrandt's parents, who posed swathed in oriental costumes. In 1631, Rembrandt left for Amsterdam and Dou established himself on his own in Leyden, where he gradually built up a great reputation. He painted portraits and genre pictures with great care; he was so meticulous that he lived in fear of the speck of dust which might fall in his paint. His pupils were numerous. Among them were Metsu, Frans van Mieris and Brekelenkam.

### JAN VAN GOYEN – 1596–1656

Born in Leyden, died at The Hague. He travelled in France and visited London. The painter who influenced him most at the beginning of his career was Esaias van de Velde, brother of Willem van de Velde the Elder, who taught him to compose pictures enlivened by peasant or military scenes in bright colour harmonies. But gradually Van Goyen renounced this brilliance; about 1627 we find his palette reduced to a few colours which he employed in very thin washes, contenting himself with a few brilliant touches. At the same time, he became concerned with painting the sky rather than figures. Van Goyen's art exercised a great influence on his contemporaries and not on the landscape artists alone. He drew from nature, as we know from four collections of drawings which may be compared with Claude Gellée's *Livre de Verité*.

### Frans HALS – 1580–1666

Born at Antwerp, died at Haarlem. He was Carel van Mander's pupil, but does not owe much to this charming mythographer. He had twelve children, of whom five became painters. He died in poverty. His early days were typical of a breathtaking virtuoso who juggled with volumes, who cut and thrust at painting with a zeal hitherto unknown. But his last works, the group portraits of the Governors of the Haarlem Almshouse, which are in a bitter and satirical vein, show that, at the age of eighty-four, Frans Hals was able to overcome all academic rules and achieve an extraordinary veracity.

### Jan Davidsz. de HEEM – 1606–1683/1684?

Born in Utrecht, died in Antwerp. He was his father's pupil, and like Van Beyeren, worked in Leyden under the influence of Pieter Potter. His work is the link between the Flemish still-life (in Antwerp he admired the pictures of Daniel Seghers) and the Dutch still-life – the link between the richness and decorative sense of the one and the meticulous realism of the other. His pictures always express a joyous plenty, but they remain in good taste.

### Jan van der HEYDEN – 1637–1712

Born at Gorinchem, died at Amsterdam. When Hobbema was an inspector of weights and measures, Van der Heyden was in charge of street lighting and fire fighting in Amsterdam. This did not prevent him from travelling, since he visited all the towns in the Low Countries and many Rhineland cities. His landscapes are sometimes exact descriptions of a place; at other times, the picture is a free composition of a castle from Germany, a church from Rotterdam and a town hall from Delft or Dordrecht, of which he had carefully sketched the most minute details. As a good realist, he does not forget a single detail, but he knows how to play with light and to give his work, no matter how diverse its elements, a perfect harmony.

### Meindert HOBBEMA – 1638–1709

Born and died at Amsterdam. There is a mystery in Hobbema's life. It is said that he stopped painting about the age of thirty. He was the pupil and friend of

Jacob van Ruisdael, but did not have his many-sided genius. He became attached to certain subjects like the water-mill, and repeated them incessantly, catching them at different times of the day. He was an impressionist before the word was invented.

### GERRIT VAN HONTHORST – 1590–1656

Born and died at Utrecht. He was the son of a designer of tapestry and a pupil of Abraham Bloemaert. He went to Italy where he studied Italian painting. In 1628 Charles I summoned him to England and he painted portraits of members of the Royal Family. He was above all a portrait painter and, although his work was uneven, he excelled in the art of chiaroscuro. *treatment of light + shade in painting.*

### PIETER DE HOOCH – 1629–1683

Born at Rotterdam, died at Amsterdam. He was the pupil of Nicolaes Berchem, a landscape painter enamoured of the Italian style, but his true master lived at Delft: he was Vermeer. De Hooch is almost exclusively a painter of interiors which he shows in clear perspective. In Amsterdam, having separated from Vermeer, he enlivened his bright, silent paintings with picturesque figures.

### JAN VAN HUYSUM – 1682–1749

Born and died at Amsterdam. Son and brother of painters, he became extremely famous for his flower-pieces, which he painted with expert exactness – almost like a botanist. His landscapes are less numerous; he composed them in his free time and peopled them with nudes.

### WILLEM KALF – 1619–1693

Born and died at Amsterdam. He travelled as far as Paris and perhaps even to Italy. Kalf began with small genre pictures in which he showed kitchen, washtub and larder. He went on to paint big still-lifes which made him famous and in which some have discovered Rembrandt's influence. These are works of great richness, but they are distinguished from the paintings of De Heem and Van Beyeren by a nobility and discretion in which we can recognise a great painter with a wonderful sense of stagecraft.

### JUDITH LEYSTER – 1609–1660

Born in Haarlem, died at Heeurstede. In Haarlem she was the devoted pupil of Frans Hals. In 1636 she married the genre painter Jan Miense Molenaer and became famous in the field of the portrait and genre scene, in which she gave proof of her verve and wit.

### NICOLAES MAES – 1632–1693

Born at Dordrecht. He was in Rembrandt's studio in Amsterdam from 1648 to 1652. He then returned to his native city, worked in Antwerp and died at

Amsterdam. Like Gerard Dou, Maes did not remain susceptible for long to the strange poetry of his master; he turned very quickly to sentimental scenes and to young girls at their windows, whom he painted, it is true, with contrasts of light and shade, but without sacrificing anything to his overriding desire for realism. At the end of his career, he developed an elegant style of painting, producing fashionable portraits which seem rather unexpected from his brush.

### Frans van MIERIS the Elder – 1635–1681

Born and died at Leyden. He was the pupil of Gerard Dou, who called him 'the prince of his pupils'. His first works are merely replicas of his teacher's paintings, although the light in them is more intense. But he succeeded in freeing himself from this influence, in enriching his palette and in developing his sense of light. He became at least as well known as Dou and had many admirers – he had four patrons in Leyden alone. His sons and grandsons, Willem, Jan and Frans, continued his manner respectfully.

### Caspar NETSCHER – 1639–1684

Born at Heidelberg, he came to the Low Countries when very young. He was the pupil of Ter Borch and came under the influence of Gerard Dou and Frans van Mieris – that is to say he painted in an elegant manner. If he did not attain the refinement of his masters, he knew how to model his volumes in light to perfection. His paintings are portraits and genre scenes of good society.

### Adriaen van OSTADE – 1610–1684

Born, lived and died at Haarlem, where he was, together with Brouwer, a pupil of Frans Hals. That is to say, to begin with, he painted in grey and, since he devoted himself to painting peasant and inn scenes and to taking us into the schools of his time, he did it with considerable zest and gentle malice. Later he became less preoccupied with the picturesque. Proof of his admiration for Rembrandt and Van Goyen is to be found in canvasses in which the transparency of colour is more important than anecdote. Finally, he returned towards more accurate story telling, but retained from the earlier period the taste for contrasts of light and shade. He even attempted to break away and to paint open-air scenes. In this medium he showed remarkable gifts.

### Paulus POTTER – 1625–1654

Baptised at Enkhuizen, died at Amsterdam. He worked in the principal Dutch towns and in the course of ten years produced a considerable number of paintings and etchings. He was at first a documentary painter who studied cows or horses with the curiosity of a veterinary surgeon. But he was able to place his accurate studies of the different breeds of Dutch livestock in a beautiful light and to capture the calm of water-meadows.

### REMBRANDT Hermansz. van Rijn – 1606–1669

Born in Leyden, died at Amsterdam. Pupil of Jacob van Swanenburgh and Pieter Lastman, he left Leyden for Amsterdam in 1631, where he was at first very successful. Three great works stand out in his career and mark its stages: the height of his fame – *The Anatomy Lesson* (1631–1632); the public's first reservations – *The Night Watch* (1642); his failure – *The Conspiracy of Claudius Civilis* (1661). Rembrandt lost his wife, Saskia, in 1642, Hendrickje Stoffels in 1662 and his son Titus in 1669. He died overwhelmed by bereavement and poverty.

### Jacob van RUISDAEL – 1628/1629?–1682

It is known of Ruisdael that he was born at Haarlem and died in Amsterdam; that he came from a family of painters of which his uncle Salomon van Ruysdael was the most famous. It is also known that he travelled in Germany and the Low Countries and that he took his 'Doctorate of Medicine' at Caen at the age of forty-eight. In short, hardly anything is known of the life of the greatest Dutch landscape painter.

### Roelant SAVERY – 1576–1639

Born at Courtrai, died at Utrecht. His first works were under the influence of 'Velvet' Breugel and Bosschaert, as is evident from his still-lifes and from his landscapes dotted with animals. The Emperor Rudolf II made him come to Prague, and of the mountain scenery he saw there Savery brought home paintings and drawings to which his present fame is due. They reveal a dramatic temperament and place him in the first rank of seventeenth-century landscape painters.

### Jan STEEN – 1626–1678/1679?

Born and died at Leyden. He was trained in Haarlem, Utrecht and The Hague. Two of his teachers are famous, Van Ostade and Van Goyen, whose daughter he married. He has been called a debauchee because he painted a number of drinking scenes. He actually drew an income from a tavern in Delft and kept an inn at Leyden, which gave him ample picturesque subjects.

### Gerard Ter BORCH – 1617–1681

Born at Zwolle. Died at Deventer. He was formed as an artist by his father and by Pieter Molijn. In Haarlem he came under the influence of Frans Hals. He visited England (1635), the court of Philip IV of Spain, France and Germany. His first pictures are of military scenes; but once the wars were over, Ter Borch painted tranquil interiors of a great sobriety. The background is barely indicated, and attention is focussed on the gleam of a material, or the reflection of light in a jewel. These are delicate, silent scenes, out of the sun, in which bright colours gradually replaced the greys so dear to Frans Hals, without robbing the paintings of their delicacy and discretion.

## WILLEM VAN DE VELDE THE YOUNGER – 1633–1707

Born at Leyden, died in London. He was formed as an artist by his father, who was also a marine painter. Dutch painting had its animal painters; it also had specialists in portraying ships. The sailors had to be able to recognise their ships and their rig. But the painter was not satisfied with looking at them in port: he went to sea. And, like a camera-man today, he was present at naval battles. The war between Holland and England did not prevent Charles II from inviting Van de Velde to London and engaging him as court painter. Besides, this naval reporter was more than merely a faithful copyist: he showed great accomplishment in painting the flat calm and the unexpected gust of wind.

## JAN VERMEER VAN DELFT – 1632–1675

Born and died at Delft. Hardly anything is known of Vermeer's life apart from the dates found in the town archives: marriage in 1653 and membership of the Guild of St Luke in the same year. His works, which are not numerous, were sold at high prices and he was twice honoured with the presidency of the guild. But everything else is guesswork. The name of Vermeer was forgotten and his paintings were despised for two centuries, until in 1866 the art historian Thore-Burger drew attention to his work.

## PHILIPS WOUWERMAN – 1619–1668

Born and died at Haarlem, he travelled in Germany, Italy and France. He was formed as an artist by his father and by Pieter Verbeeck, a painter of horses. He was certainly, if indirectly, influenced by Frans Hals. His two brothers painted hunting scenes, battles and landscapes; he was a painter of horses which he treated, like Potter, with obvious attention to accuracy, but he made slightly more attempt than Potter to enliven the canvasses with picturesque scenes of huntsmen and cavaliers.

PLATES

*ROELANT SAVERY*
FLOWERS. 1624
Central Museum, Utrecht

*FRANS HALS*
THE JOLLY TOPER
Rijksmuseum, Amsterdam

*FRANS HALS*
THE GIPSY GIRL. 1625
Louvre, Paris

55

*FRANS HALS*
BANQUET OF THE OFFICERS OF THE ARCHERS OF ST GEORGE. 1627
Haarlem Museum

*FRANS HALS*
HILLE BOBBE. 1655
Staatliche Museen, Berlin

57

*GERRIT VAN HONTHORST*
INCREDULITY OF ST THOMAS
Prado, Madrid

*JAN VAN GOYEN*
Château de Montfort. 1645
Thyssen-Bornemisza Collection, Lugano  59

HENDRICK AVERKAMP

WINTER LANDSCAPE
Rijksmuseum, Amsterdam

61

*JUDITH LEYSTER*
THE GAY COMPANY. 1630
Louvre, Paris

*ADRIAEN VAN OSTADE*
THE FISHMONGER. 1661
Wallace Collection, London

*PAULUS POTTER*
HORSES GRAZING. 1694
Rijksmuseum, Amsterdam

*NICOLAES MAES*
Young Girl at the Window
Rijksmuseum, Amsterdam

*PIETER DE HOOCH*
DUTCH INTERIOR
National Gallery, London

*PIETER DE HOOCH*
WOMAN WEIGHING GOLD
Staatliche Museen, Berlin

67

*GERARD DOU*
REMBRANDT'S MOTHER. 1631
Rijksmuseum, Amsterdam

*REMBRANDT HARMENSZ. VAN RIJN*
THE ELEVATION OF THE CROSS. 1633
Alte Pinakothek, Munich

69

*REMBRANDT HARMENSZ. VAN RIJN*
SELF-PORTRAIT WITH TURBAN AND GOLD CHAIN. 1634
Louvre, Paris

REMBRANDT HARMENSZ. VAN RIJN
THE NIGHT WATCH. 1642
Rijksmuseum, Amsterdam

*REMBRANDT HARMENSZ. VAN RIJN*
THE PILGRIMS AT EMMAUS. 1648
Louvre, Paris

*REMBRANDT HARMENSZ. VAN RIJN*
WINTER LANDSCAPE. 1645
Staatsgalerie, Cassel

73

*REMBRANDT HARMENSZ. VAN RIJN*
LANDSCAPE WITH A COACH. 1645
Wallace Collection, London

74

*REMBRANDT HARMENSZ. VAN RIJN*
PORTRAIT OF AN OLD MAN. 1654
Hermitage, Leningrad

REMBRANDT HARMENSZ. VAN RIJN

THE SYNDICS OF THE CLOTH HALL. 1661
Rijksmuseum, Amsterdam

*JAN VERMEER*
A STREET IN DELFT. 1685
Rijksmuseum, Amsterdam

*JAN VERMEER*
MAIDSERVANT POURING MILK. 1658
Rijksmuseum, Amsterdam

79

*JAN VERMEER*
GIRL DRINKING WITH A GENTLEMAN. 1660
Staatliche Museen, Berlin

*JAN VERMEER*
THE LOVE LETTER. 1664
Rijksmuseum, Amsterdam

*JAN VERMEER*
LADY STANDING AT THE VIRGINALS. 1670
National Gallery, London

*JAN VERMEER*
THE PEARL NECKLACE
Staatliche Museen, Berlin

*JAN VERMEER*
THE GUITAR PLAYER. 1667
The Iveagh Bequest, London

ABRAHAM VAN BEYEREN
STILL-LIFE
Rijksmuseum, Amsterdam

*CASPAR NETSCHER*
THE LACEMAKER. 1664
Wallace Collection, London

*JACOB VAN RUISDAEL*
RAY OF SUNLIGHT
Louvre, Paris

89

JACOB VAN RUISDAEL
STORMY SEA
90       Thyssen-Bornemisza Collection, Lugano

*GERARD TER BORCH*
LADY AT HER TOILET
Wallace Collection, London

*FRANS VAN MIERIS*
PORTRAIT OF A YOUNG WOMAN
Thyssen-Bornemisza Collection, Lugano

*WILLEM KALF*
STILL-LIFE
Louvre, Paris

93

*JAN VAN DER HEYDEN*
THE AMSTERDAM CANAL
Louvre, Paris

*WILLEM VAN DE VELDE THE YOUNGER*
THE SALVO
Rijksmuseum, Amsterdam

95

*PHILIPS WOUWERMAN*
THE WHITE HORSE
Rijksmuseum, Amsterdam

*AELBERT CUYP*
MOUNTAIN LANDSCAPE
Rijksmuseum, Amsterdam

*MEINDERT HOBBEMA*
THE WATER-MILL
Louvre, Paris

*MEINDERT HOBBEMA*
THE AVENUE AT MIDDELHARNIS. 1689
National Gallery, London

99

*JAN VAN HUYSUM*
STILL-LIFE
Wallace Collection, London